T0203207

Dedication

"With gratitude to God

for my dear family:

Eric, Johanna,

Björn, Karl-Jon and Isabel"

to

from

Meditations for Mom
Copyright © 2018 Bonnie Sparrman

Published by KPT Publishing
Minneapolis, Minnesota 55406
www.KPTPublishing.com

ISBN: 978-1-944833-36-7

Cover/interior design by Koechel Peterson and Associates,
Minneapolis, Minnesota.

Scripture quotations marked (NIV) are taken from THE
HOLY BIBLE, NEW INTERNATIONAL VERSION®, NIV®
Copyright © 1973, 1978, 1984, 2011 by Biblica, Inc.® Used
by permission. All rights reserved worldwide.

All rights reserved. No part of this publication may be
reproduced, stored in a retrieval system, or transmitted in
any form or by any means—electronic, mechanical, digital,
photocopy, recording, or any other—except for brief quotations in printed reviews, without the prior permission of
the publishers.

First printing April 2018
10 9 8 7 6 5 4 3 2 1

Printed in the United States of America

Meditations for
Mom
by Bonnie Sparrman

KPT PUBLISHING

Contents

INTRODUCTION

The word "mother" is a verb. Because mothers are constantly *doing*! We carry, teach, comfort, bathe, snuggle, bandage, rock, protect, feed, love, discipline, hug, and—eventually—release our children. Mothers have so much to do each day, it's a challenge to prioritize which needs come first. Of course, "mother" is a noun as well. Mothers are walls of safety and doors of opportunity for our children. Some days we are event planners, other days we are financial counselors. Mothers are mediators, chauffeurs, psychologists, cooks, mechanics, nurses, and IT specialists. And despite the thousands of times I've reminded my messy brood that I am not the maid, I have certainly been both cleaner and keeper of our house. So many of these energy-sapping tasks are never complete. When my kids were little, I preferred mowing the grass to doing laundry because the lawn would be done for an entire week. (The fact that I couldn't hear any cries or complaints over the din of the lawn mower was a secret benefit.)

As frequently as you may feel like an invisible servant, keep in mind that mothers are the nurturers of tomorrow's adults. When you drag your weary self out of bed to feed a screaming baby in the night, you may not feel convinced that being a mother is a very high calling. But it is! The sacred task of mothering is an integral part of a journey of faith. And as you or someone you love faces the ridiculous challenges, the gut-wrenching heartaches, and the hilarious joys of raising children, it is my hope that this book will encourage you and cheer you on.

At our wedding ceremony, the pastor (who happened to be my future father-in-law) made the audacious comment that children may some day come along to *bless* and *challenge* us. I felt my face grow hot, its crimson hue contrasting starkly with my white dress. My father-in-law's hopes for us became reality six years later, when my husband, Eric, held our firstborn—our baby girl Johanna. Her brothers, Bjorn and Karl, followed quickly, and, years later, Isa came into our home as an exchange student. We had four teenagers sharing one bathroom and one computer. Now *that* was a challenge. But we wouldn't have had it any other way.

To encourage people is literally to "provide them with courage." Through this book I hope to give mothers some courage for the exhausting, daunting, but incredibly rewarding task of being a mother. Our job description as mothers is vast and varied and asks us to reinvent ourselves every few years. May we spur one another on as we serve God by serving our families.

I love being a mom and have journaled about its joys and challenges for years. When the workload generated by three kids aged three and under became intense, I had less time to write. So my husband bought me a tiny voice recorder so I could still collect my thoughts. I remember one desperate "journal entry" that was nothing more than closing myself into our bathroom for a good long scream into my little microphone! I thought I'd hit the wall that day, but once again, God's grace was real to me, and I emerged from the bathroom to be "Mom" for a few more hours—until bedtime came at last.

This is not a how-to book for parenting. Rather, it is a collection of honest reflections on how Christ blesses our days as we face the many thankless details of raising children into the world. While the job of mothering is unglamorous much of the time, its rewards are eternal.

You should know beyond anything else that you do not mother alone. While the responsibilities feel weighty and require wisdom that stretches our souls, God is good and gracious and loves us every step of the way. Not only is Jesus our guide and inspiration, He is our light during the darkest nights and our companion along the bumpiest roads. Sometimes His presence appears through people who hearten our weary spirits on dismal or difficult days. Other times, He speaks to us through the beauty of His creation. And, always, He offers strength through His Holy Word.

It is my earnest prayer that every mom who needs her heart buoyed may find God in these simple words. May you draw close to Him and rejoice in His care for you. You are lovely in His sight, even if you have sacrificed smooth legs, a flat tummy, or perfectly manicured nails to have and to hold your children. Cosmetics are temporary. But the energy, creativity, enthusiasm, and oodles of love that you shower on your children will have results that are never-ending.

Through the years, our family has been spoiled by an annual vacation with friends who walk a few steps ahead of us down the road of parenting. They have already raised two boys into wonderful young men. Now they chuckle as they watch my husband and me deal with the antics of our squirrely kids. If one of our boys challenges me, our friends back me up by telling him, "Your mom is right. It says so in *The Handbook*." If we annoy the boys by reminding them to dress warmly or embarrass them by prompting a more audible "thank you," our friends refer to the rules of *The Handbook*. Our kids jokingly hear, from other parents as well, that their mom and dad are *supposed* to annoy and embarrass them. It's an inevitable part of our job as we raise them. This so-called *Handbook,* much to the kids' consternation, has been my ally now for many years. They ask, "What is this *Handbook*? Who wrote it? Where can I get a copy?" As they have been told, they do not get a copy until they are parents themselves.

So, to my dear friends who mother, my advice is to arm yourselves with *The Handbook,* whatever your version of it may be. Let it be your invisible helper, as it has been for me. Add it to your arsenal of survival tools, along with prayer, God's Word, and strong friends to share your burden. And when you feel yourself getting weary, down, or disenchanted with any of numerous challenges life hands you, remember the promise that God offers you in Isaiah 40:29–31 NIV:

> *He gives strength to the weary*
> *and increases the power of the weak.*
>
> *Even youths grow tired and weary,*
> *and young men stumble and fall;*
> *but those who hope in the* LORD
> *will renew their strength.*
>
> *They will soar on wings like eagles;*
> *they will run and not grow weary,*
> *they will walk and not be faint.*

You, too, are a child of God. May you feel His love each day and His strength each hour.

But you are a forgiving God,

gracious and compassionate,

slow to anger and abounding in love.

Nehemiah 9:17

The World's Worst Parents?

The dog poops on the carpet one time too many; your fourteen-year-old rolls her eyes and sasses off, and the boys are wrestling on the living room floor. You're stressed because your house defines "pandemonium," and guests will walk through the door for dinner in less than two hours. You've had it with your house looking like a rummage sale, with everyone leaving clothes, shoes, CDs, baseballs, books, and dishes randomly strewn about. The kids' rooms look like grenades went off in their closets. You've tried to be patient, but you feel an uncomfortable pressure building in your gut. And then it happens.

You blow. You spew one verbal assault after another until your darlings clearly realize that Mom has reached the end of her rope. As your words splatter against one and all, you realize they sound eerily similar to something from the past. Where have you heard this before? Oh yeah, you've just become a reincarnation of the worst version of your own mother. AHH! The kids collect their belongings faster than candy on Halloween, dart out of the line of fire, and eye you suspiciously for possible aftershocks.

As soon as this happens to me, I *know* I have over-reacted, and I feel terrible remorse. While a clean house is lovely, it's not worth terrorizing its inhabitants to get there. But loosing my cool over housekeeping isn't the only reason I'm a guilty parent. It's just the beginning. I've often been impatient and too hard on the kids. I have not always listened when they need to talk. I carry regrets. I'm sorry I didn't insist that a musical son get the lessons he wanted. But, fortunately, I know I'm not alone in these mistakes—or any others.

Several years ago my husband and I began a dinner group with friends. We meet once a month to eat and to pray with one another. It didn't take many gatherings before we realized that most of our conversations and prayers revolve around the lives of our children and the challenges of parenting. We admit our mistakes. We all had to laugh when we realized that over and over we discuss how we think we have blown it with our kids. Eventually we dubbed ourselves the WWPs. Our collective pile of kids knows what it stands for: the World's Worst Parents.

From time to time we all fear that we are the world's worst parent. We worry that we have done our children permanent damage. What do we do with the knowledge of our shortcomings and regrets? Here are a few suggestions gleaned from years of gatherings with my fellow WWPs:

- As parents, we all blunder from time to time. Confess not only to God, but when appropriate, to the kids, too. This teaches them how to apologize, and lets them see you as a fellow human being who is trying to do her best. Remember that God forgives and has more grace for you than you probably do for yourself.

- Go easy on yourself. The first child is a complete experiment. (So is the second, and the third, and the fourth etc.)

- Look back and see that as you put your trust in God, He is making progress in your life and also in the lives of your kids. Thank Him and move forward.

- Guilt is not of God. Conviction is. Let go of guilt, lest it wear you out.

- Pray for your own personal growth as a mother. Let God cultivate your heart.

- Get together with other parents you respect and pray for your families together.

Eric and I are wholeheartedly grateful for our friends who share this journey of parenting. At times, God has given insights about our own kids through the observations of our friends, who have a more objective view. Sometimes, we are too close to a situation to discern what is happening in our own homes, and a close friend can shine a light on what seems utterly confusing to us. Frequently, we howl with laughter as we share the wild tales of raising kids, and sometimes we are reduced to tears. Both are valid and go a long way to lift our hearts. We really get a kick when the kids come into the dining room only to quickly slink away because they've caught us praying for them. This may cause some momentary embarrassment, but I'm glad our kids know that people other than their own mom and dad hold them securely in prayer.

The wisdom that

comes from heaven,

is first of all pure:

then peace-loving,

considerate, submissive,

full of mercy

and good fruit,

impartial and sincere.

Peacemakers who sow in peace

raise a harvest

of righteousness.

JAMES 3:17-18

A Word for the Wise

If moms don't need wisdom, I don't know who does. Have you ever counted how many decisions you make in one day that have both short- and long-term effects on your children? The number of choices we face on their behalf is staggering, especially when children are young. But as they mature, we need wisdom to encourage *their* blossoming decision-making ability. How do we know what is best?

In the Bible, God tells Solomon that He will grant him one wish. Imagine having the God of all history, the God of heaven and earth, giving you whatever you ask for. It's better than a magic genie in a lamp. Solomon could ask for all the wealth, comfort, and power that were available in his day. But he doesn't request a Mediterranean cruise, a bigger mansion, faster horses, or a longer life. Instead, Solomon admits to God that he is like a little child who doesn't know his way around. He asks God for wisdom. And God is so pleased with his request that he gives Solomon great wisdom posthaste. Suddenly, others clamor to hear the king's wise words. When the Queen of Sheba arrives with a list of questions to test the king, she finds herself impressed and humbled and departs his palace praising him as the wisest person she has ever known.

While you and I aren't necessarily striving to be the smartest mothers ever known, God does want to share wisdom with us. But it's important to remember that being wise is different from having a head full of information. Information helps you be a prudent shopper and pay bills. But wisdom comes from experience and involves using good judgment. I have spent years trying to discern the best educational choice for my children. Public school? Private school? Home school? Virtual? Some combination thereof? These arduous decisions drive us to our knees as we implore God for wisdom, a sign, or a message. I've wished in vain for a hot air balloon to float overhead with God's clear answer emblazoned in bright colors. God works in more subtle ways than that, but His Holy Word says it all. As the Bible says in James 1:5, "If any of you lacks wisdom, he should ask God, who gives generously to all without finding fault, and it will be given to him."

Just remember wisdom won't just arrive via a hot air balloon. It grows out of years of discipline and self-control. We absorb knowledge by brushing shoulders with those who are more experienced than ourselves. In the same way, we grow in our knowledge by "brushing shoulders" with God and His followers. Working alongside some impeccable chefs has allowed me to learn from their expertise. They have blessed me with their skills and sound judgment. And by spending time with faithful women and more experienced mothers, who have cried through deeper and darker nights than I, I've gained insight as well as community.

And what I learn is that wise mothers don't rely on themselves, their husbands, or their friends for everything. When all else is stripped away, it is God who holds up the ground on which we stand. So let's plant our feet and trust in our trustworthy God to help us through every easy, difficult, or impossible day.

*T*rust in the LORD
with all your heart and lean
not on your own understanding;
in all your ways acknowledge him,
and he will make your paths straight.

PROVERBS 3:5-6

Unexpected Outcomes

As mothers, we hold in our hearts expectations of how our children will turn out. It's only natural. Because my son was the always the tallest in his class, many assumed he'd be wonderful at basketball. While he loved "hoops" as a little guy, that interest was quickly overshadowed by his passion for art and music. As a high school senior, he spent his time throwing pots in the art studio rather than throwing a ball in the gym. That's who God made him to be: a potter/painter/blacksmith/drummer/guitar player who happens to be tall. His talents were not up to me, and while they suit him well, they're not all "typical." I did not expect that Bjorn would prefer slamming a hammer on an anvil to slam-dunking a basketball. But my son is incredibly successful at what he's chosen to do. The thing that needed adjusting was my own expectation for him.

As we all know, there are times when parents have to back off and let young-adult children decide how they will live and what they will do each day. Our daily tasks of making sure they are well-fed and dressed warmly enough are over. But what do we do when they choose to live differently than we had hoped? If they are not living up to their abilities? If they make a poor choice in their education? With friends? With a marriage partner? With their life in general? This is a tough struggle in the heart of any mother.

Mothers pour their energy, their love, and their very lives into raising children who may eventually make poor choices. These can be dark valleys indeed. Obviously, we can't control our grown children. We can't change the way they think, the way they respond to their friends, or the way they hear our words of concern. So what's a mother to do?

Every single wise mother who has dealt with adult children on a circuitous route tells me that they have tried to stop themselves from seeing their children as possessions—that God entrusts them to our care for a time, but not forever. They cling to conviction and prayer—diligent prayer for their children. Of course, this requires immense faith and perseverance. When children disappoint, we don't stop loving them. In fact, letting them know we love them—and that God loves them— is really important.

In moments of disappointment, it is only natural to feel deep sadness as we remember all the sacrifices we've made and the years we've dedicated to raising a son or daughter well. If a child isn't living up to his or her potential, it's easy to be bitter about the pain this causes. But it's not about us! Sure, we want to be proud of our children. And, for the most part, our children want to make us proud. We humans are a complicated bunch—flawed, vulnerable, capable of making great mistakes—but also capable of great humility, understanding, and love.

But more than that, it is about our faith. Will we trust in God with all our hearts, and lean not on our own understanding? Will we acknowledge Jesus in all our ways so that He, in His infinite wisdom, will direct our paths?

Loving, learning, and letting go of our children is a journey of great faith. It's one of the most difficult journeys a mother will take. As mothers, we must remember that we are not required to raise children who do not make mistakes. We are required to be faithful. We're required to love our children unconditionally, as we have been loved by God. We're required to let them go when it's time, but we are never required to let them go emotionally. We'll always keep them in our hearts and in our prayers. That's just part of what it means to be a mom.

*H*old on to instruction,

do not let it go;

guard it well, for it is your life.

PROVERBS 4:13

To Teach Is to Learn

I'm sure you've heard the words that the best way to learn something is to teach it. How true! Each time I teach a cooking class, I learn something new that I didn't understand as well before. Reviewing information or skills to a point of complete comfort effectively hammers concepts into our brain. While you and I learned many things as children, so much is forgotten. The good news is that as we teach our children, we benefit by learning all over again—and hopefully this time it will stick!

As mothers, we are caught up in teaching our kids everything we can—from manners to money to reading to writing to tying their shoes to driving a car. But the kids aren't the only ones who are learning. While your child is behind the wheel for the first time, who is learning self-control and patience under pressure? Your white knuckles may give away your terror, but you learn to remain calm as the car lurches too close to the curb or—worse yet—toward oncoming traffic. Talk about having to put faith into action!

Has being a mom taught you, as it has me, how much you like to be in control of your days? Have you realized yet, as I have, that having control is virtually impossible? While I may wrestle for control with my family, I learn more and more that I really can't control much at all. A well-scheduled week may be blown off the pages of my calendar as quickly as a neighbor's child gets sick, the car breaks down, or a friend calls with bad news. Eventually, we learn to give up the need to control everything as our calendars remind us that life sometimes has a mind of its own. As our children grow in skills and knowledge, it is good to know that God is growing us as mothers too. I am glad that God is honing my mind and heart through the years. It is exciting to look back and realize that faith is not static, but dynamic, as we trust in Jesus as our teacher. He is knowledge and wisdom. As we draw ever closer to Him, He is able to teach us, and help us grow into stronger women.

Difficulties that may have caused you considerable stress years ago don't affect you in the same way anymore. That's noticeable progress. I have a dear friend who, when under great stress, could be found crying at the back of her closet with a bottle of wine and a bag of cheese puffs. Now with many more years of experience and many more layers of faith, she responds to stress in much more productive ways. Have you ever asked the question, "What does mothering teach me?" What have you learned as a mother that you might not have learned any other way? For me, mothering works like a tenderizer on the heart. I can be tough in all kinds of situations, but when it comes to my children needing care, understanding, healing, or forgiveness, I am soft. I am quick to come crawling when one of my little ones needs God's help. This teaches me that God is always there, always real, always diligent in his goodness . . . if I only remember to ask Him for help.

So do not fear,

for I am with you;

do not be dismayed,

for I am your God.

I will strengthen you and help you;

I will uphold you with my

righteous right hand.

ISAIAH 41:10

Hurting Child, Hurting Mom

Good news indeed to settle in your mind, since the quickest way to hurt a mother is to hurt her child. Are you with me? Most mothers would gladly take the place of their offspring who may be the victim of anything from bullying to illness to heartbreak. Our hearts are woven so deeply and mysteriously with our children's that we identify deeply with their pain. We feel it keenly and make it our own. As a mother, your heart is capable of enormous love for your child, to the point of feeling severe suffering within yourself. As with anything that requires such unswerving dedication, motherhood makes our hearts more vulnerable to being trampled— or at least aching—when our kids have been treated unfairly or struggle against terrible odds.

My husband and I know a young woman whose mother must have been acquainted with deep pain, as her daughter struggled with even the simplest aspects of life. Lena Maria was born without both arms and half of a leg. We met Lena Maria while she toured the U.S. singing concerts. She was a guest in our home, where we enjoyed meals together. She easily lifted her glass to drink and handled a fork with such dexterity that one completely forgot she had no hands. Eating is just one thing. She either walks with a prosthetic leg or bounces on her strong leg. With the help of a passenger to turn the key, she drives. She can do almost everything else necessary to live independently—and to go beyond. Lena Maria has won many medals for swimming in the Special Olympics. She is a real champion.

Yet for all these accomplishments, it's hard to imagine the pain Lena Maria's parents have known while watching her struggle. When asked how her parents handled her handicap, she explained that her mom was very wise to not give undue help as she grew up. When it was time for Lena Maria to dress herself, her mom patiently stood back and let her wiggle into her clothes so she could achieve her own independence. How painfully difficult it must have been for her mom to not intervene! But how insightful she must have been to realize that by letting Lena Maria struggle, she was helping her to become stronger. To Lena's own credit, she thanks her parents for allowing her the freedom to wrestle with her limitations.

I'm not suggesting that we leave our children alone in terrible situations to battle every challenge for themselves. But there are times when our children are up against agonizing situations that we simply can't fix. So what's a mother to do?

A mother I know has a daughter who struggles with depression. She tells me it is a journey of faith. It is a letting go of our children every hour into the hands of God. It is gut-wrenchingly painful, but as we love our children through winding paths, our faith grows accordingly. The deeper the waters we swim, the deeper we can know God's love and depend upon His care. I am not suggesting this is easy or that we would ever choose to grow closer to God through difficulties. But I do believe that He never leaves us nor forsakes us, no matter how impossible life feels.

I thank God for His reassuring words in Isaiah 41:10: "So do not fear, for I am with you; do not be dismayed, for I am your God. I will strengthen you and help you; I will uphold you with my righteous right hand." Good news indeed to settle in your mind as your head meets the pillow and your soul needs rest.

Whoever wants to become great

among you must be your servant,

and whoever wants to be first

must be slave of all.

MARK 10:43-44

The Invisible Mom

Moms practice many occupations as we care for our busy broods. This morning I am an ATM producing quick cash, a short-order cook making hot breakfast, a chauffeur, a laundress, a nurse dispensing medications, and an errand girl picking up a fresh supply of everything—from pencils to produce. Later today I will be a gardener, and then a proofreader for one who is writing a paper. Sometimes, I am an amateur psychologist, counseling one of my kids or one of their friends. I'm also a baker, saving us from having to consume peanut butter between white sponges. Occasionally I'm a seamstress, a travel agent finding the cheapest way for the kids to get back to college, and a cheerleader at cross-country meets. Grocery shopping requires me to be a nutritionist, reading ingredient labels. And every day we moms are teachers, whether we realize it or not.

While the variety of jobs is mind-boggling, it's not always stimulating for the brain or appreciated by the darling offspring who live in our homes. Do you ever feel like the invisible mom constantly pouring yourself into task after task, hardly able to remember that you once read classical literature or studied for college exams?

When I remember the bygone days of being a student, I feel like I'm recollecting another person whom I only read about. Was it really me?

It is easy to forget who I am when thankless, mundane chores abound from morning 'til night. I've been known to smirk and sigh when someone prays over a meal, thanking God for "the hands that prepared it." My sarcastic little brain quips, "Yep, just the *hands* that prepared it. Forget the brain that researched the recipe, purchased or grew the ingredients, and remembers the perfect temperature at which to pull the salmon from the grill!" I suspiciously eye the ungrateful eaters who don't really appreciate that I am more than a pair of hands created to serve.

While the anonymity of being the invisible mom can feel exhausting, the list of chores seems relentless. Many tasks feel unimportant. Compensation by the world's standards isn't great, since any tips are limited to the occasional quarter that rattles around in the bottom of the dryer. And verbal thanks aren't always forthcoming. So what keeps us mothers going?

How about the fact that we are in the business of helping shape the next generation of teachers, engineers, artists, physicians, builders, scientists, economists, leaders, and—above all—parents? All of the mundane tasks that require your organizational skills, your energy, your intellect, and your creativity are actually doing a holy work. We are more than "the hands that prepared" the laundry, the meal or the morning medicine.

If you are a mother, God has called you to the awesome task of grooming one or more of His children for service in His kingdom. I honestly can't think of a higher calling. The loads of laundry and the most uninteresting list of chores are just little pieces of the puzzle. It encourages me to remember that God *calls us* to be servants! In Mark 10:43–44 Jesus says, "Whoever wants to become great among you must be your servant, and whoever wants to be first must be slave of all." This sounds contrary to our spa-obsessed, make-me-comfy society. I don't mean that we can't enjoy a pedicure. (I'd love one!) It just reminds us that being a servant is a noble calling, too, and is worth every bit of our creative energy and effort.

Serving our children well also includes passing the batons of laundry, cleaning, pet care, gardening, baking, banking, trip-planning, and any chores that growing kids are able to do. Teaching them how to accomplish the myriad housekeeping tasks we've been accustomed to doing will equip them well for moving into that dorm room or first apartment—or first home with their husband or wife. Of course, it can be easier to just mop the kitchen floor yourself, but gleaming tiles isn't the only goal. Raising children who can also perform a task and appreciate the results is even more important. So, blessings on you as you serve—and teach your children to serve as well. We may feel invisible now, but our efforts will be evident for generations to come.

*B*ut seek first his kingdom

and his righteousness,

and all these things

will be given to you as well.

MATTHEW 6:33

The Hunt

We all have a few pet peeves that trounce our last nerve. My top two have to be oversleeping on a beautiful morning and losing things. In both situations, something is lost. To oversleep is to lose out on a lovely morning walk or a perfect cup of coffee. To lose an object is to have lost both the object and the time it takes to hunt for it.

Unlike scavenger hunts or fox hunts, the hunt for a lost object is not a chosen sport. In fact, it is a dreaded activity abhorred by the head of the hunt (me). Have you ever noticed that Mom is most often the person called on to know the whereabouts of shoes, library books, home-work papers, retainers, soccer shorts, permission slips, and mustard in the fridge? To be "Mom" is to be omni-scient. Like me, you may have outfitted your home with places to keep such items, but whether it's due to lazi-ness, lack of sleep, or just plain life—things get lost.

Many years ago, it was our goal to leave for a trip at 6:00 a.m. This was our usual strategy, which got us out of Washington D.C. before the morning traffic. Unfortunate-ly, one little red high-top tennis shoe went missing the day before the planned departure. This pair of shoes was three-year-old Karl's only pair that fit at the moment. *All night* I searched, absolutely certain that it was in the house. Not only was the shoe lost, so was my entire night of sleep, which hurt the next day when I was activity director for the thirteen-hour drive to Michigan. The shoe was finally discovered a year later behind an old chest of drawers in the basement. It no longer fit.

Many things have been lost in our household since the red high-top, providing many opportunities to analyze the process of the hunt. It goes like this. At first I don't want to admit that the misplaced piece of paper or wristwatch—i.e, the Lost—is truly in the category of Seriously Missing. Denial abounds. After a five-minute glance in the usual places, it dawns on me to question everyone in the family for their eyewitness accounts. If they look at me stupidly, I rev up my efforts and rifle madly through papers or a pile of books that were whisked out of view the last time we had company. If the Lost still eludes me, I begin the mental part of the search. This involves thinking through the last time the Lost was used or seen. It does not involve haphazard moving of stuff; it involves retracing steps and exercising memory.

If the Lost is still not recovered, my pulse increases and my frustration rises. I chastise myself for allowing such disorganization to exist under my roof. I become critical of family members who may have responsibility for any part of the Lost being lost in the first place. I look at my watch and calculate how many precious minutes are spent searching, registering my frustration with any listening ear.

Finally, I get spiritual. I pray, beg, and plead with God that the Lost will magically appear before my eyes so I don't go completely insane. My heart is simultaneously nagged by the thought that a lesson is to be learned via the hunt. At the moment the search and rescue is successful, I rejoice, thank God, and promise to straighten up any disheveled corners of the house.

In retrospect, I can clearly see the stages of this frustrating, self-inflicted process: something is lost; I deny it. Next I try to find it quickly by myself. That being unsuccessful, I try *harder* to find it by myself. Then, much to the frustration of my family, I both blame them for the loss and recruit them to help. When I'm finally ready to tear my hair out, I get the God of the universe involved because I remember that He knows where everything is.

Through many search-and-rescue operations, this is what I have learned:

1. God wants me to rely on Him *first*.

2. He reminds me to ask Him early in any hunting expedition what He is trying to teach me. (Sometimes, I learn that I need a serious house cleaning!)

3. It is better not to blame others for misplacing things because *I* might be responsible.

4. I need to be patient with helpful young hunters lest they get wounded in the hunt.

5. And here's the kicker. Jesus is also in the business of hunting. He is the Shepherd who goes out and searches fervently for even one lost lamb. If you are ever separated from God, He longs to find you and carry you back to safety. And when one little lamb—or person—is found, God and the angels in heaven have a party to celebrate his or her homecoming.

So, next time you are the lead hunter, talk to God early on. Your frustration over something that is lost may bring you to the Lord, who is the ultimate expert on searching and finding and bringing lost things to light.

Be still, and know that I am God.

PSALM 46:10

"Sit Down and Shut Up"

When I asked a friend what words I'd need most to teach high school students, she replied, "Sit down and shut up!" Wow, I thought, those last two words aren't even allowed in our house. But the more I sat with them, the more their meaning sunk in. Just as students need to be quiet in order to hear their teacher, we need to sit down and keep still before God so we can hear His voice and sense His spirit. We need to allow God to be our counselor by listening for Him in the midst of our busy days.

I know this can be an extremely difficult thing to do when you have children in your care. When our kids were all under five years old, when every hour was broken down into nanoseconds, I remember promising to give God my full attention for my first five minutes of free time (if I ever got any) during the day. Getting three little ragamuffins to nap at the same time was like trying to line up the stars, moon, and planets, but some days the seemingly impossible happened. When it did, I'd grab my Bible, flop across our bed (my version of sitting down and shutting up), and give God a chance to speak. I'd pour my heart out to Him, begging desperately that our quiet moments not be interrupted. Sometimes, I fell asleep while praying, which met another important need. Oftentimes, as five minutes turned into more, God's presence and reassurances from His Word became a balm to my soul. In hungry exhaustion I read, "God is our refuge and strength" (Psalm 46:1). "Be still, and know that I am God" (Psalm 46:10). "Come near to God and he will come near to you" (James 4:8). This is great news for any over-taxed mother!

We all know that finding moments of quiet in the day is difficult at best. One mother I know resorted to climbing into her young child's crib, the only place her toddler didn't want to go, so she could nab a few moments of peace. Before things get that desperate, here's an idea I've tried with success. Write a particular verse from the Bible on a sticky note, and then keep it in a visible place throughout your day. Whether it's on the handle of your child's stroller or on the dashboard of your car, meditating on it while you are in the trenches can be a life line. No matter how crazed you've been with the tasks of motherhood, God hasn't taken His eyes off you for a moment. He is far more gracious with us than we are with ourselves.

We need to remember how richly God blesses us when we make ourselves available to hear His extraordinary, strength-giving voice. Time you spend with God is never wasted. At times I've been sorry I've spent too long on the phone or procrastinated while shopping, but I've never wished I hadn't spent so much time in prayer. The time we spend with Jesus helps hold us up when our spirits are weary. Five minutes with Jesus may be the most nourishing, best-spent time in your entire day.

*L*et the morning bring me

word of your unfailing love,

for I have put my trust in you.

Show me the way I should go,

for to you I entrust my life.

PSALM 143:8

Refuel

A s we all know, mothering takes oodles and oodles of energy. And I don't just mean physical energy when kids are young. Emotional, mental, and spiritual stamina are tested again and again as mothers, in a single day, make about as many decisions as an air traffic controller. The tedium of relentless problem-solving can really take it out of a gal, and without a plan for refueling, we can find ourselves too tuckered out to be much help to anyone, let alone ourselves or our families. I've been there. How about you?

I am a people person, but I also need solitude to clear my head long enough to think, pray, and reach deeply into God's Word. At times I have had to perform ridiculous feats to carve out a few moments alone. Each summer, we vacation at a beach cottage where one creaking door will signal to the kids that the grown-ups are up, and the day has begun. But I so long for time to read, write, pray, and run and jump into the lake early in the morning that my strategy is now to place my swimsuit, journal, and Bible next to my bed before going to sleep. In the morning, I silently slip into my suit, lift the screen, and climb out the window onto a carefully placed lawn chair directly below the windowsill. I run to the beach feeling momentarily free and more like one of the kids myself. These are important times. Times to refuel. Times to read. Times to be reminded of God's promises that He'll be with me no matter what the day, the month, or the year may bring.

One morning at the beach I discovered Psalm 143:8, which has been a great encouragement to me ever since. It says, "Let the morning bring me word of your unfailing love, for I have put my trust in you. Show me the way I should go, for to you I lift up my soul." Such fantastic words wrapped God's sovereign love around my heart with perfect timing, as that summer we were contemplating a cross-country move that felt scary and overwhelming to me. I had put my trust in God, but to be reminded again in a very personal way that His love was with me and that I could ask Him to show me the way was a great comfort.

Believe me, most of my mornings don't start near a beautiful beach or with the freedom to climb out a window to forty minutes of youthful freedom. But whatever our circumstances or whatever our location, we constantly need to be refilled, refueled, and reenergized.

Here are a few ideas for recharging that have served me well over the years:

1. Make a coffee date with a friend who really cares about you.

2. Take a walk in the woods, or through a field, or in a park, or if you are especially fortunate, near some water. Breathe deeply.

3. Take your Bible and some lovely stationery to a coffee shop. Read a while and then write a letter to a friend.

4. Dress up and meet a friend for tea or for lunch out.

5. Rent an inspiring movie. Watch it with a favorite beverage and a special snack.

6. Do something creative! Bead a necklace, arrange some flowers. Browse the library or bookstore shelves.

7. Read a new magazine.

8. Call an out-of-town friend whom you've been missing.

9. Go shopping without a stroller.

10. Take a bubble bath without little people.

I realize that many of these ideas require a babysitter. If you can't hire one, swap babysitting with a friend who is as desperate to get out as you are. Or rely on a spouse or a grandparent, real or surrogate. While I've never had the luxury of a parent even remotely close by, I've been extremely blessed with people who love my kids and have been willing to take care of them in order to give me a break. Often, the children will remember their fun outings with these generous women and men as much as I treasure my precious time alone.

Refueling of any sort comes at a cost. Just remember that you won't run any better on empty than your car. And while it's expensive at the pump, it's not worth it to discover you're out of fuel while cruising the interstate.

*R*ejoice always; pray continually—

give thanks in all circumstances;

for this is God's will for you

in Christ Jesus.

1 Thessalonians 5:16–18

Praying for Our Children

It took serious effort to muscle our stretch stroller up the hill with our bobble-head toddlers in pajamas all ready for bed. This was our last walk of the day, with the intent to induce a quiet journey into the land of nod. My husband commented this job was getting difficult—our three growing kids hardly fit in the stroller anymore. My quick comeback went something like this: "Are you kidding? Difficult? All three kids are in the vehicle that *we* control! We choose where to go and we decide when to return home. It will never be this easy again!" And I meant it. I prayed that we would savor every wonderful day of these early years that I sensed were racing at break-neck speed to stages far more precarious.

At that moment with the stroller in our hands, we did have a considerable amount of control over our children's lives. But even then, control is like smoke—you can't hold on to it. And on that peaceful summer evening with our freshly bathed, bunchy babes all snuggled against each other in their carriage, I nervously anticipated the day they would have bigger wheels, minds, and plans of their own—and the volumes of prayer that would necessitate. As time went on, the stroller was traded for tricycles,

tricycles for two-wheelers, and . . . you know where it all leads. One day quite recently, our six-foot five-inch son folded and stuffed his gangly frame into a small and weary car for a trek across town. Our daughter currently hangs over the Atlantic on her way to study abroad. My prayers follow them again and again.

Perils of the road and the air are not the only reasons to surround and uphold our children in prayer. While it may take a lifetime to begin to understand the necessity and mystery of imploring God to watch over, protect, lead, guide, and surround our children, I believe it is one of my most important endeavors as a mother and as a follower of Jesus. Whether they leave for school a mile down the road or fly off to foreign lands—or even practice piano where we can hear them—I can't help asking God to lend His blessing and presence to their lives.

My greatest desire for our children is that they will joyfully love and follow Jesus Christ all their lives. After that, the grocery list includes prayers for their health and safety, relationships, future spouses, decisions about studies, careers, and their character development. I also pray that if they are up to trouble of some sort, they will be quickly found out.

The prayers of mothers and grandmothers are powerful forces of goodness in the lives of those they pray for. As a middle school student, I was impressed to learn that my pastor, whom I considered a strong and great man, still depended on the prayers of his mother as he did his work every day. I have also known people who, as hard as they resist, cannot avoid being caught in the net of Jesus' love only to find out that their mothers, grandmothers, and friends have frequently brought their names up to God in prayer.

Scripture reminds us over and over to bring our needs and requests to God in prayer. James 5:16 says, "Confess your sins to each other and pray for each other so that you may be healed." First Thessalonians 5:16–17 says, "Be joyful always; pray continually, give thanks in all circumstances, for this is God's will for you in Christ Jesus."

Interestingly enough, praying not only benefits those we hold up in prayer: we who pray discover our hearts are drawn closer to God and into deepening intimacy with Him. Just as conversation is necessary to feed any relationship, the steady habit of talking with God entwines our hearts closely with His. He wants us to depend upon Him. He waits patiently for us to call.

So, fellow moms, as we drop our kids off for school, let's pray. As they come home after a long day, let us continue to pray that we will be sensitive to their needs. In all they do, from playing to studying to sleeping, let us uphold in prayer the precious ones whom God has entrusted to our care.

I rest peacefully knowing He loves my children even more than I am able to do myself. And wherever they are, when I have prayed specifically for them, I know that God is watching over them, and He holds them in the safety of his arms.

Be strong and courageous.

Do not be afraid;

do not be discouraged,

for the LORD your God will be

with you wherever you go.

JOSHUA 1:9

Overwhelming Responsibility

My heart soared when I realized I'd survived the birth of our first child! As tears and sweat poured over my face, my heart was awash in triumph, elation and relief. The power of these emotions was new for me, but I'd seen many other mothers go through birth, so I knew that the expected, optimal outcome usually included both a shrieking baby and tears of relief. What I didn't expect was the next feeling that took me completely by surprise. As the doctor handed over our screaming, wiggling, red newborn baby Johanna, a sense of responsibility like I had never known before flooded over me like a giant wave at the beach. She weighed only 7 pounds 6 ounces, but she felt so heavy to me. I didn't think I was prepared to be that responsible. I felt terribly inept, and while tears of joy rolled down my cheeks, my heart quaked with a strange new sense of needing to learn what it meant to be a parent, a mother. How would I know what to do with this completely beautiful, but completely helpless, little human?

In those few poignant moments after the birth, my mind raced forward like a movie trailer, playing through the joys and challenges that would certainly fill and forever change our future years. I tried to take in the newness of this role of mother, caregiver, and the one on whom nourishment, teaching, and life itself would greatly depend. My husband was there as well to share this responsibility, but I knew quite a lot of it depended on me as the mom. I poured my heart out to God, asking for His help to raise and love this little girl the way He wanted me to. I begged for wisdom, knowing I would need a lot. And I prayed for my trembling, tiny, warm wonder, that she would quickly know God's love for her, and know beyond the questioning of her teen-age years that His love is for real, for every day and for all time.

We don't mother alone. We don't need to carry this heavy responsibility by ourselves. Even a single mother isn't raising children by herself. The God of the universe promises to be with us, granting wisdom, strength, and even some moments of rest as we press on and trust in Him. None of us can accomplish the tasks of mothering alone. Sometimes, we moms try to carry too much of the responsibility by ourselves when we could find willing help in family, friends, our church, and sometimes even professionals. We are no less capable or loving when we admit we need assistance.

In these times, allow God's grace and peace to pour over you and fill you with His encouraging spirit. When your giant platter of obligations feels topsy-turvy because you've let it become overfilled, it's important to ask God what ought to be omitted and what is truly necessary. When He lifts the burdens of certain tasks that I like to do but aren't necessary, He graciously reminds me that this busyness is only for a season, and not forever. Someday the garden will look better, and I will revisit my weaving loom. But for now, my self-imposed standards are pared down to the bare-bones, important priorities.

As wildly demanding as motherhood can be, God's heart of love and grace is able to keep up, and to help us keep up too. The responsibilities will not suck you under the current. Rather, lean on your Heavenly Father who sees, hears, and cares when you cry out to Him for help. I like to remember a little plaque that hung in my bedroom when I was little. It said, "He cares for you" (1 Peter 5:7). I've carried it with me in my mind's eye ever since. Because I know that it is true.

*O*ffer hospitality to

one another without grumbling.

I Peter 4:9

Multiplication, Not Addition

Have you ever noticed how the number of children in your house doesn't stop with however many happen to be your own? With each additional child, the total count for dinner or for beds multiplies as each one increases the circle of friends they wish to include. While planning extra food, extra seats in the car, and more bunks for our kids' pals is stressful, what a blessing it is to get to know these friends and to extend our hospitality to them.

With three in high school at one time, our home has been especially chaotic, with a constant parade of teen-agers piling in and out, leaving their mountain of shoes at the door, their milky glasses in the sink, and various shoes, T-shirts, books, and backpacks around for me to trip over and sort out.

Tuesday afternoons stretch my tolerance, as that's the day our son's band practices in our basement. Sometimes, I struggle to form a complete thought as they produce enough noise to incur complaints from the neighbors and prevent any chance of using the phone. In fact, if your child ever shows an interest in drumming, just say NO and offer a trip to Europe instead! In pre-band days I didn't realize that drum sets are not very mobile, thus most bands practice at the drummer boy's house, at the expense of drummer family ears. Ah, yes, pop around our place any Tuesday afternoon—you'll smell the fragrance of cookies baking and feel the cacophonic throb from below.

The fragrance of cookies, you ask? Absolutely! Just in case this noisy foursome ever think of taking their music to a bigger, better, or nicer venue, it's my intent to keep them at our house by appealing to their growling after-school tummies. We have a great relationship of supply and demand. I bake, they eat! I know where our kids are, and I know whom they are with. Yeah, it's a bit hard on the nerves, and I run out of chocolate chips a lot, but that's a small price to pay to know these wonderful musicians who fill our house with joyful noise! Keeping our door and our hearts open to the friends that our kids bring home is a privilege.

I know a wonderful mother who constantly extends hugs, a listening ear, and a place to sleep to teens in the neighborhood whom others misunderstand due to the length of their hair and possibly the way they smell. Her home is a haven where the welcome mat is out at all hours of the day and night. When she mothers the ones whose mothers may not be available, she brings Jesus' love to kids who need it most. And while these teens come around for food, acceptance, laughs, and the warmth of a home, they also know they'll hear trusted words of advice or admonishment from a mom who remembers what it's like to be seventeen.

This mother does what the Bible says in Romans 12 when Paul advises, "practice hospitality." What that really means is welcome strangers and foreigners. Let me tell you, some of those teenagers look strange and seem foreign, yet they are welcomed and loved, which is why they keep coming back.

So we mother the children God gives us, and we can mother the ones He drops at our doorsteps . Either way, kids find love and acceptance, which is what God wishes for His children. May He strengthen you and give you discernment as you care for children you know who need a mother's love.

*H*er children arise

and call her blessed.

PROVERBS 31:28

Mud Pies and Kites

Having kids is the best excuse I know to play like a child and do something completely worthwhile at the same time! Being a mother has its perks. How else could I justify countless hours playing in our kids' sandbox, making forts out of cardboard boxes, shaping clay, leading hiking expeditions, building snowmen, sledding, flying kites, making mud pies, climbing trees, and building with blocks? I haven't had so much fun since I was a kid!

At the end of a day when my work involves being home with the kids, my husband asks, "What did you do all day?" I've been known to sheepishly reply, "We built an enormous zoo out of blocks, complete with a train, animal hospital, and water feature. We baked cookies for our tea party under the spruce tree and took naps in our cardboard castle in the basement. We read books on the top bunk and made pancakes that look like teddy bears, and we ran through the sprinkler, which is why the floor is all wet. And dinner isn't quite ready; we have been really busy!"

At moments like that, I feel a twinge of guilt knowing that my husband was in meetings, taking phone calls, and handling hundreds of details of his job all day long. I, on the other hand, was goofing off with the kids. He is kind to remind me that it isn't just goofing off. Spending time actually playing with our kids is investing not only in them, but in future generations. Playing with our children builds a strong relationship with them, which is invaluable. Even doing tasks alongside a child is a wonderful way to be engaged with them while teaching them important skills. This sometimes requires the patience of a saint, but in the long run, it pays off.

I love to bake. Generally, I love to bake by myself, because I can be orderly, efficient, and I don't lose track of measurements. But I have baked in chaos alongside my children since they were eighteen months old, when I brought the ingredients and mixer down to their child-size table. Even little hands can toss carrots in olive oil, knead dough, break eggs, and, with help, scoop and measure flour, sugar, and salt. My boys distinctively scooped all dry ingredients front-end loader style complete with boy noises. Now, as young men, they are proficient bakers and cooks.

While passing along skills to our kids is valuable, we can't underestimate how much this nurtures our bond with our children. Obviously, we can't play with them all the time, but when we take the time to enjoy their activities and invite them to be a part of ours, we know each other so much better.

On the other hand, I have observed many a mother who ostensibly "spends time" with her little ones by going on a stroller walk or to the pool, only to chat on her cell phone nonstop. I have watched kids grab their mother's face and pull it toward them while she continues her conversation into the all-important phone. She's there in body, but that's it. I fear the day will come when that child has mastered her behavior, and the mom won't have to worry about the child wanting her attention anymore. Texting and chatting will be the center of their relating.

So Moms, let's connect with the kiddos and have a little fun! Blow up a beach ball; blow some bubbles. Your kids will giggle to see their mom having such a great time jumping in leaves or crossing a stream on a log. They aren't impressed by our sophistication, but by our playfulness. Any kid prefers Mom in Saturday play clothes to her dressed-up look! My kids say I look best in my jeans and polo shirt with my hair in a ponytail. The truth is, I look the best in their eyes because it means I'm home with them! I know it is a luxury even to have time to hang with the kids. And while it's less restful than a lunch date or even going to my job, it's energy well-spent and well-enjoyed, with positive eternal consequences.

Someday, your children will stand and bless you in return for the fun-loving attention that you lavished on them when they so desperately needed it.

*C*arry each other's burdens,

and in this way you will fulfill

the law of Christ.

GALATIANS 6:2

Mothering Is Not a Solo Tour

Solitude for mothers of small children is nearly as difficult to orchestrate as world peace. Creative wrangling of circumstances is required even to be allowed the privilege of going into the restroom unaccompanied by a small cherub. Showers become family events, and sad to say, luxuriating quietly in the bathtub may be a vague memory or a rare treat savored only on Mother's Day. Our admiring, loving little ones want Mommy—not a substitute. Since finding solitude long enough to know how you're feeling on a particular day may require a stroke of genius, isn't it ironic that in the confines of all this closeness with another human being, we can be overcome with loneliness?

Mothers try to make it on their own all too often, only to wind up feeling isolated and desperately alone. Mothering shouldn't be a solo tour! During the demanding years of trying to instill the best we can into our children, we need relationships for ourselves that encourage and support us. We may spend much of our days talking, but constantly answering a three-year-old's question of "Why, Mommy?" about every passing cloud, insect, and truck just isn't the same as conversing with a friend. Relationships are either filling or draining, and while it is very fulfilling to have a relationship with your child, being the constant caregiver can also leave a mother depleted in body and spirit.

I remember feeling particularly alone one day as I toted our three preschoolers to the playground near our home. The usual banter of mother-child and child-child musings followed us up and down the slide and back and forth on the swings. My crew was a chatty bunch, and while I loved talking with my knee-high detectives, I longed to chat with a friend.

God certainly blessed me that day in the park, because along came another mother with a little guy about the size of my boys and a baby girl tucked in the crook of her elbow. I had not seen her before, but our kids almost immediately started racing around together. As it turned out, she was new to the neighborhood, having just left her friends and family many states away. She had an upset stomach and had asked for a plastic bag for the long walk home. I happened to have one and handed it over without delay. Providing is what moms are good at, and, anyway, who wouldn't feel compassion for a woman exploring a brand-new home, has two little ones to care for, and feels as though she might throw up? Considering her condition, it wasn't the time for deep conversation, but I felt like I'd met a new friend. A few days later, I introduced myself to her husband, who thanked me for the sick bag and for being kind to his wife.

I thought, *Are you kidding? She was there for ME!* God knew that I needed a friend who was into play dates and Jane Austen novels. Shelley invited me over for cappuccino and cinnamon rolls. It turned out to be the first of many such invitations. Sometimes, we got together for collective mending sessions. We stitched and chatted while our kids built box forts in the basement. Occasionally, on a birthday, we'd escape for afternoon tea that lasted much longer than our husbands could fathom. Her friendship filled a void that my husband, as dear a friend as he is, couldn't fill. When we're mothers, being friends with other mothers is invaluable to our survival.

Since then our babies have grown to be adolescents and young adults, and we have both moved to different cities in distant states. However, to this day we are the best of friends who continue to share book titles, hand-me-downs, tips on keeping our sanity, exercise plans, heartaches, accomplishments, disappointments, strategies for communicating with teenagers and—very importantly—prayer requests. On very rare and special days, we still manage to rendezvous for a visit that includes afternoon tea and a marathon chat. The concerns we share have changed over the years, but we still need to talk as much as ever. This convinces me that mothering requires friendship no matter what stage we are in. Galatians 6:2 says, "Carry each other's burdens and in this way you will fulfill the law of Christ." Do yourself a humongous favor; ask God whom you might befriend. You may discover a kindred spirit to share with you in the depths and the heights of life.

The LORD is my shepherd,

I shall not be in want.

Even though I walk through

the darkest valley,

I will fear no evil,

for you are with me;

your rod and your staff,

they comfort me.

PSALM 23:1, 4

Monsters Under the Bed

To be a mother is to know fear. Much like things that go bump in the night, our fears can be much bigger and more powerful when sleep ought to be the activity of the moment. Fear is the monster under the bed, and if it happens to wake me up, the worry center in my brain gets stuck in the "on" position, and my mind conjures up ridiculous topics of worry—as if I didn't have enough valid concerns.

It's easy to wonder whether we're able to meet all the needs of everyone who depends upon us, let alone ourselves. You might stew, "Will I have time for my husband AND children? Am I a good mother? Will I teach my child what he or she needs to know to become a contributing member of society? Will I effectively encourage my child to have excellent character? Will we be able to afford raising our kids? How about college? Will my child choose faith in God? Will parenting preclude an adult social life forever? What if my child becomes ill or has an accident? What if my teenager totally rebels? When my twenty-year-old leaves for a foreign country, will she be safe?"

In the depths of the night, even when tucked snuggly in bed, with all the kids under our roof, my mind can be too busy firing off alarming unproductive thoughts. I'd like to bundle them up in old rags, soak the pile with gasoline, and light a match to it. My fears would be consumed by a blaze of brightness, and I would be free to lie down again in peace and tranquility without these enemies tormenting my mind. But since the smoke and fire would only pass anxiety and worry along to my husband, I must choose another strategy altogether.

Sometimes, I have searched my mind for peaceful places. I'll remember when I was little at the beach with my family, or it was Sunday afternoon dinner with my grandparents—attempting to relive pleasant times and situations. But then I start missing them, and everyone who is not with us anymore, and I feel like crying. That's when my pea-brain finally reaches the end of its tormented rope and settles down to something solid.

I start reviewing words that God has handed right to me through Scripture. The most comforting words that I have committed to memory from the Bible come from Psalm 23. They are my survival during a thunderstorm, a root canal, or a night rattled with fears. The LORD is my shepherd, I shall not be in want. He makes me lie down in green pastures, he leads me beside quiet waters, he restores my soul. He guides me in paths of righteousness for his name's sake. Even though I walk through the darkest valley, I will fear no evil, for you are with me; Your rod and your staff, they comfort me. You prepare a table before me in the presence of my enemies. You anoint my head with oil; my cup overflows. Surely goodness and love will follow me all the days of my life, and I will dwell in the house of the LORD forever (Psalm 23:1–6).

Sometimes, I fall asleep before I even get to the darkest valley. Sometimes, I have to think it through several times, but it always reminds me that I am not alone, and that what takes place for us here on earth is not the end of it all. We have love and goodness to follow us through the days of our lives, but even better than that, we will live forever in the house of the Lord! The words of this Psalm give peace and rest when both attempt to elude us. Even if it's not copied to your brain yet, equipping your bedside with this Psalm and a little flashlight may prove more powerful than you can imagine.

When pride comes,

then comes disgrace,

but with humility comes wisdom.

PROVERBS 11:2

Moments of Mortification

M-O-M. Those are the three important letters that I remember struggling to print perfectly on Mother's Day cards when I was a little girl. She was the woman who wore pretty aprons in our kitchen, pedal pushers in the backyard, and lovely dresses on Sundays. But she was so much more than that. She was my caretaker. She was my teacher. She was my M-O-M.

Then I became the recipient of those precious cards with the word Mom scripted carefully in crayon surrounded by drawings of flowers and butterflies. I treasure such expressions of my children's love for me, and at times have stared in wonder at the word "Mom," still feeling a bit surprised that it refers to me. Shocking thought. More recently I've giggled to realize that the word "Mom" is also a handy acronym for the humbling experiences that cause us mothers to shudder with embarrassment. I call these the "Moments of Mortification." If you have a child past infancy, you know exactly what I'm talking about. We are called to survive many of these mortifying moments as we raise our kids.

Recently I was walking with a friend who has always been pleasantly open with me about the shenanigans that her now-grown sons lived through and put her through. "Yes, it makes a mother proud," she said a bit sarcastically after relating a tale of her son involving the police, a false ID, and an attorney. Ah yes, those moments of mortification, when our hearts aren't exactly soaring like they did at kindergarten graduation. As we crossed a bridge I couldn't help draw her attention to the only graffiti gracing its surface; an intricate logo in bright red, black, and white. "Makes a mother proud," I said as we stood contemplating the interesting design. She cracked up, guessing correctly that the artist must be my oldest son whose style of expression is unique and recognizable. "Yes," I commiserated, "real proud."

The heart of a mother races with pleasure when her son or daughter is recognized for a job well done, or wins the race or takes a bow to an auditorium filled with enthusiastic applause. For that moment our worth and goodness are wrapped up with our offspring's. Their success feels like ours. "That's my daughter; the one who looks like me. She really does sing beautifully, doesn't she?"

But oh how the same heart will plummet when a teacher's phone call begins with the words, "I regret having to relate this negative report about your son so early on a Monday morning, but at the school event last Saturday . . ." At such a moment we hope and pray that the teacher has inadvertently called the wrong parent so we can be above such painful blows to our ego—and go on thinking our child is above such reproach.

I've experienced both ends of the spectrum: utter joy at a child's accomplishments, and sheer exasperation at their willful blunders. I notice that the latter causes me to shy away from the school office and the high school staff, avoiding the cheerful greetings I'd share with them on a better day. What is it in me that causes that change in behavior?

It's my abominable pride! I am thinking too much about myself and how I feel. It's ridiculous! My pride is downright sinful. Do I feel drawn to other moms whose obedient kids and shiny lives seem absolutely put-together, like a beautifully wrapped birthday present? Of course not. Likewise, I've actually sensed that friends and acquaintances find me more approachable when they know that our home and our lives aren't so pristine.

So while the moments of mortification can be painfully embarrassing, they serve to keep us humble, which is how God would have us be. When we're humble, He can use us better to encourage others. We also tend to throw our hurting, honest souls toward Jesus, relying on Him for our purpose and worth. Proverbs 11:2 reminds us that "when pride comes, then comes disgrace, but with humility comes wisdom." I'd rather have wisdom any day.

Our identity as mothers is not wrapped up in our child's benchmarks of success. We all desire that our children do well, but a kindergartener's reading level, ability on the soccer field, or grade point average are not measures of worth, either the child's or our own. Rather, our God takes us while we are hurting, humbled, mortified, soaring, or truly heartbroken and tells us that in Him, we are worthy.

Let the little children come to me,

and do not hinder them,

for the kingdom of God

belongs to such as these.

MARK 10:14

The Fountain of Youth

In a great story of the Bible, people bring little children to Jesus to be blessed. Unfortunately, Jesus' disciples don't appreciate this show of faith, and they make their disapproval apparent. Jesus is indignant with His disciples' behavior. In Mark 10:14 He says, "Let the little children come to me, and do not hinder them, for the kingdom of God belongs to such as these." He even pushes His message a step further and elevates the position of children by adding, "Truly I tell you, anyone who will not receive the kingdom of God like a little child will never enter it."

Have you ever wondered why Jesus says we need to be like little kids to receive His kingdom? What is it about children that shows us what Jesus desires in His followers? He does not say we are to be like fathers or mothers or any wise elder or senior statesman. No, He clearly says we are to be like little children, turning conventional wisdom on its head.

When we are mothers of very young children, we have the privilege of seeing firsthand why Jesus states this preference. We're able to observe the wide-eyed amazement of our kids as they discover the world bit by bit each day. We hear them ask pertinent questions, sometimes to our complete exhaustion as we attempt thoughtful answers to the relentless flow of "why, Mommy?" and "how, Mommy?"

One day at a pond hidden in some woods, my son asked in all sincerity, "What are frogs for?" Ah, frogs. I was speechless for a moment trying to think of a good answer, when his wise older brother of three years got me off the hook with his clear and emphatic answer, "They are for praising God!" Zing! Great answer. Why didn't I think of that? I agreed wholeheartedly and again pondered how my knee-high boys showed more insight than I did.

My son may possibly have been told in Sunday School that everything on earth, the great trees, all the animals, forests, lakes, meadows, and mountains, is here to praise God. And he believed it. His acceptance of this concept illustrates another attribute about small children that I believe Jesus wishes for us: children are naturally trusting. They expect us to tell them the truth. They have not yet learned to be cynical, jaded, or doubting like adults. Eventually, we want them to question and wrestle with issues for themselves, but as little children, it is fine for them to trust, to accept, and to believe.

Similarly, Jesus wants us to trust Him, to accept Him, and to believe in Him. He wants us to trust Him with our every need each day. And unlike people who can be too moody or too tired to really listen, Jesus is constantly available. He wants to both listen and offer His wisdom, forgiveness, and steady love. When we are like little children running to Him for comfort, He so willingly takes us up into His lap and blesses us as He blessed those dear children over two thousand years ago.

Don't you think Jesus is also pleased by the utter enthusiasm shown by little children? When a loved one comes home, kids run with wild abandon into a loving embrace. Later, they wrap themselves tightly around the legs of the one they love who is trying in earnest to leave. They clearly show their likes and dislikes. They are completely honest, uncomplicated communicators. How refreshing.

Oh, how Jesus longs for us to run to Him because we trust He is our strength and our hope. He waits for us and wants to bless us with His loving touch. May we never be too grown up or too sophisticated to exuberantly accept the love God offers.

A cheerful heart is good medicine,

but a crushed spirit dries

up the bones.

PROVERBS 17:22

Might as Well Laugh

Wham! A small but strong hand thumped me on the head, and I was instantly awake. I was also instantly irritated with our youngest (and at the moment, hungriest) boy, who wanted his breakfast and told me so—loudly. He had wisely figured that until Mommy was out of bed and into the kitchen, getting food was out of the question. He was doing his best to speed up the process. Although I didn't appreciate being pummeled into consciousness so early in the morning, the seriousness of his desire to eat made me giggle. I also found it something of an honor that he knew exactly where to come. So instead of expressing my exasperation, I took Karl's little two-year-old hand in mine and very gently stroked my head where he had hammered it moments before. I told him that he could wake me up any time he needed me, if he would be gentle and whisper. Then I got up, and we headed downstairs to eat.

Sometimes, when you feel like screaming in frustration at the antics of your precious children, you can look for the silliness in the situation and find yourself stifling a laugh instead. None of us enjoy mud on the carpet, messy bedrooms, squabbling siblings, or teenage boys who mumble instead of speak clearly. But look for the humor in the situation. Honestly, if you don't laugh, you'll go crazy! I am convincing *myself* to opt for this angle, because all too often I take my frustrations too seriously, which doesn't do anyone in the family any good. Sometimes it's easier to do this in retrospect, but even then, a good belly laugh truly puts joy in our hearts.

Here's a good one. On our church's first Sunday in a new building, I was teaching sixth grade Sunday School. One of our clever students mysteriously wore his winter parka to class even though it was 98 degrees outside. When his jacket antics became a distraction to the class, I asked him to please put it out in the hallway. His strong resistance should have tipped me off to mischief, but it didn't. Finally he obeyed. Not thirty minutes later, several people were horrified to discover a rather large white rat running free in the church! This boy's father was perturbed when he found out why he was pulled from the class he taught, but since then we have all laughed uproariously about the rat that came to church in a boy's jacket.

Keep in mind that the most frustrating experiences of raising children actually create family folklore that keeps everyone in stitches through the years. I know some rambunctious boys who ran through a bedroom door with a broom handle. Mom pulled off a quick fix by suddenly installing a full-length mirror on one side and a large poster on the other. Dad didn't know about it until ten years later, when the house was being painted before a wedding. His response? He didn't want to know what else happened while he was at work. This same family also left their ten-year-old at O'Hare airport! He was eventually retrieved, and the story lives on. Another story: when my brother-in-law was in the fourth grade, he needed bubble gum so badly that he snuck out of school to buy it at the grocery store. Unfortunately, he didn't see the store's clean plate glass window and walked right through it, raining down glass on his head. He was a hero at school, but his mom didn't see the humor until the scene was a safe distance in the rearview mirror.

Remember that Proverbs 17:22 says, "A cheerful heart is good medicine, but a crushed spirit dries up the bones." Choosing cheerfulness over a crushed spirit takes effort. Naturally, we don't rejoice when disasters strike in our homes. It doesn't take much for a boy's curiosity, a magnifying glass, and some dry leaves to bring out the fire department. However, it does require a lot of self-control on the part of the mother not to ground her son for life. Eventually, this incident will become the grist of a life lesson for the boy, his siblings, and his parents, who chose cheerfulness and love over anger. And someday, when this young man is a father, his tale of pyrotechnics will be a story he can use to teach his children responsibility.

As far as my little early morning noggin boxer, ever since the day I showed him how to gently rub my head and ask for breakfast in a whisper, he has! And I've never known a sweeter way to be awakened.

The LORD will guide you always;

he will satisfy your needs

in a sun-scorched land

and will strengthen your frame.

You will be like a well-watered garden,

like a spring whose waters never fail.

ISAIAH 58:11

God Provides

I needed these words when we moved from Michigan to a suburb of Washington D.C. with our eighteen-month-old. I was eight months pregnant, and we were experiencing stiflingly humid August weather like I had never known. We left friends, family, church, my trusted OB, the familiar hospital where I worked, and the home we dearly loved—the prettiest little bungalow near cool Lake Michigan. Our parents and siblings were now ten and thirteen hours away, and I looked like an over-ripe pumpkin. I was pretty sure we had made a huge mistake. I poured out my desperate cries to God, tried to assimilate to a new community, and hurried to find a physician whom I could trust to deliver our baby in only four weeks.

With a high number of stress points fraying my nerves, God provided for me in amazing ways through wonderful people. On our second Sunday at our new church, I met a young mom who was visiting for the first time. Our kids swam together that afternoon. Two weeks later, when I had the baby, she brought over the most delicious meal, just like I was an old friend. When I saw that beef bourguignon, salad, and an applesauce cake on my table, I knew we'd be friends for life. This mother is the kind of super-woman who knows what a girlfriend needs sometimes before she knows it herself. She brought me the love of Jesus in the form of a listening ear, and a shoulder to cry on, a clean bathroom, shared holiday meals, and many prayers.

Another surprise that could have been orchestrated by God alone took place just after the birth of our baby in the hospital I had visited only once. My nurse and I chatted as she examined our newborn. I mentioned to her that I was a newcomer, and that my mom, who was also an OB nurse, was flying in that afternoon to meet her new grandson. Come to find out, this nurse I had never met had been a co-worker of my mother's for many years in Chicago. She knew my mom! That did it. I bawled. It was as if God said to me, "I know this situation isn't what you wanted, but I know exactly where you are, and I am taking care of you." When Mom arrived at the hospital two hours later, it was a joyous and unexpected reunion.

To be so cared for and loved by family and old friends is wonderful, but to be embraced by complete strangers is to meet Jesus face to face. Although I knew no one, suddenly my kids had babysitters, playmates and adopted grandparents. You might think that was just because my husband was the new pastor. While our church was wonderfully welcoming, we also received an outpouring of care and friendship from brand-new neighbors whom we met simply because God placed them on our block. Next door and across the street, new folks moved in just after us, and we became family for one another. As one of them told me, "Friends are the family that we choose for ourselves." I agreed, and also might add, "Friends are the family God gives us when our family is far away."

My boulder-size doubts were not too big for God to shove out of the way. While I still missed my blood relatives and Midwest pals, I was not left alone or ever out of God's sight. I am not saying that to trust in Jesus means our problems will go away and we'll never fear or doubt, but I can say with every fiber of my being that He cares for you and will never leave you alone to fend for yourself.

*C*ome to me,

all you who are weary and burdened,

and I will give you rest.

Take my yoke upon you

and learn from me,

for I am gentle and humble in heart,

and you will find rest for your souls.

For my yoke is easy

and my burden is light.

MATTHEW 11:28-30

Rest Up

Most jobs are not as constantly demanding as being a mother. When I worked as a staff nurse in a newborn nursery, I had many responsibilities caring for our bunch of babies all swaddled snugly in their cozy receiving blankets. But when my shift was over, I gave report to the next crew and flew out the door feeling light and free of worries about my little charges. Several years later, my own nursery of babies was at home, and my shifts no longer came in eight- or twelve-hour increments. Yikes, this job was literally 24/7! No wonder a pediatrician's waiting room full of mothers can look like a bedraggled army between battles. When ear-splitting cries came over the baby monitor at any hour of the day or night, I often had to ask God to please give me not only the wisdom to figure out what to do next, but also the strength to do it.

Though the intense time demands ease up a bit as children grow older, mothers still lose hours of sleep over homework assignments, late-night heart-to-hearts, and kids who for whatever reason can't sleep. A sage of a mother once told me that as kids grow up, the physical exhaustion common for mothers of toddlers gives way to greater psychological exhaustion. When kids are in high school, their needs revolve around decision-making and are of a more emotional nature. How true! There are relationships to discuss, school schedules to plan, and college choices to mull over. Not to mention the nights when the whereabouts of teenagers keep our ears alert for the sounds of closing car doors or footsteps coming home. And if I hear sirens while waiting, I have been known to slip outside and even down my street making sure no harm has come near my child. This sort of night is anything but restful!

I jokingly commented to a friend as our sons graduated together that the reason so many mothers cry at graduation is because these poor women are completely exhausted. While I was partly kidding, my friend saw the truth in what I said. She had spent countless hours preparing a beautiful graduation celebration, all the while hoping and praying that her brilliant son would complete the requirements to walk the commencement exercises with his class. Not only was this mom working very hard on very little sleep, she was worried that their dream of graduation might not become reality, even though the announcements were in the mail. At moments such as these, who doesn't worry? And what mother isn't exhausted?

No time is more taxing on a mother's body and soul than when her child is injured, ill, or in danger. We offer our most earnest, fervent prayers with great force, send-ing them straight to the very heart of God, begging, plead-ing for the fever to stop, the counseling to help, the treat-ment to work, or the surgery to be successful. At moments such as these, exhaustion is the mother's plight, but she is so intensely caring for her beloved child she may not even realize it for weeks to come. And then CRASH! It all catches up.

At these moments of bone-crushing exhaustion, God in His perfect timing has put before my eyes words that on first reading made little sense to me. (I was too tired to get it and too cynical and stubborn to admit that He was talking to me.) But Jesus clearly spoke the words: "Come to me, all you who are weary and burdened, and I will give you rest. Take my yoke upon you and learn from me, for I am gentle and humble in heart, and you will find rest for your souls. For my yoke is easy and my burden is light" (Matthew 11:28–30). While mere words didn't remove the dark circles from beneath my eyes, they lifted my spirit and reminded me that Jesus was up with me when I rocked our babies in the night. He knew my desperate need for sleep, my dog-tired bones. This season would not be forever, and some day when I would be missing my finally-fledged children, I would remember how dear it was to hold them close and safe.

O Lord, our Lord, how majestic
is your name in all the earth!
You have set your glory above the heavens.

From the lips of children and infants
you have ordained praise because of your
enemies, to silence the foe and the avenger.

When I consider your heavens, the work of
your fingers, the moon and the stars,
which you have set in place,

what is man that you are mindful of him,
the son of man that you care for him?

You made him a little lower than the
heavenly beings and crowned him
with glory and honor.

PSALM 8:1-5

Connect with the Creator

At the front of the worship space in my church, through a window in the shape of a cross, I spy a limestone ridge accented by plumes of native grasses that miraculously push themselves out of pure rock. Juniper trees crown the hill in varied shades of green, and sometimes a busy squirrel scampers by while a bird soars overhead. This view changes with the seasons and the weather, fluctuating between beauties breathtaking and magnificent. My relationship with this little piece of earth has given me much to contemplate from my vantage point during church.

Sometimes, the beauty of this bit of earth washes over me like an overwhelming gift from God, catching me with such surprise that I'm unable to keep singing. Somehow, the melody of a song mingles with the shadows of the trees, and I can imagine lying on a blanket beneath aromatic branches, peacefully part of God's creation. I am reminded of a particular hike years ago, bushwhacking through the deep North Woods over beds of ferns into meadows of daisies and buttercups. It isn't wise to let my mind dwell on the memory too long, or I'll have embarrassing tears running down my face and wonder what is wrong with myself. I doubt anyone else looks out the window and cries. So what is it?

It's God! He made this fantastic, beautiful earth, and He lets us live in it! His vast creativity is evident in all of nature. His imagination stretches to infinite lengths, and my soul longs to be a part of it. If I could not see outside during worship, I couldn't worship as well. I long to be connected with God and the earth He made. From the time I was in kindergarten I have hoped for a seat by the window and made a habit of taking meals outdoors. One thing I love about our kitchen, the room we use the most, is the way the windows connect us with nature as we cook and eat, enjoying the seasons and the creatures that God has provided.

As mothers of kids who love technology, we live in an era of great separation between nature and people. Delivering kids directly to the doors of our homes and schools drastically insulates us and them from the elements and fresh air. While some technology can be just fine, why not get outside and take in God's goodness? Children are naturally drawn to the adventures our tremendous world has to offer. Acorns, sticks, brooks, mud puddles, leaves, rocks, snowdrifts, and even small hills invite children to explore. The "play house" in our yard is a mossy green cave under a giant blue spruce tree. We've hosted many a tea party in this deliciously magical space.

The influence of the great outdoors isn't so bad for moms, either. While fresh air promotes sleep for the young ones, it gives us the chance to clear our minds and praise God in the loveliness of His creation. I feel closer to God when I have taken the kids on a walk through the park or out under the darkest skies to see the amazing beauty of the Milky Way. Nature feeds our souls.

If the day is cold or rainy, remember there is no such thing as bad weather, just bad clothes. And if we do get chilly, or soaked to the skin, warming up with hot chocolate and cozy blankets is another way to feel God's love surrounding us.

Praising God for the boundless beauty of this earth He has given us is amazingly therapeutic. No matter how enormous my problems feel, they seem less significant when I lift my heart in joyful thankfulness to our Creator. In thanking Jesus for the corner of the world that He allows me to appreciate, I'm blessed with perspective and inspiration.

*B*ut the fruit of the Spirit is love,

joy, peace, patience, kindness,

goodness, faithfulness,

gentleness and self-control.

GALATIANS 5:22-23

"Good" Morning!

It was a BAD morning. And unfortunately it was also a Sunday. I resented that since becoming a mother, I couldn't even manage to make it to church with combed hair and a put-together look. But I remember that *particular* Sunday morning with horror. It took place while I was a single mother with a three-year-old, a two-year-old, and a six-month-old baby. I wasn't *really* a single mother, except on Sunday mornings, when my husband, a pastor, left for church before the rest of us began our day. Maybe if I had been a single mother every day, I might have been better at handling the children on my own, but I doubt it. I was lousy at getting the three kids and myself ready and delivered to church by the time it started.

That fateful Sunday morning, I started with the oldest, our three-year-old girl, who already held way too many opinions about her attire. We squabbled over the choice of dress and shoes, and as I began to dread her teenage years, I decided the hair bow wasn't worth a fight. I let her wear it the way she liked, pulled down around her ears looking ridiculous. Next I tackled our busy toddler, whom I wrested and cajoled into an adorable one-piece outfit. He sat sweetly on his bed-room floor playing with blocks while I fed the baby and began to dress him on the changing table. Suddenly, I was distracted by splashing sounds across the hall. To my frustrated amazement, I realized the blocks had bored him, and he moved into the bathroom, where he sat in the toilet with a toy boat, zooming a fresh wake through the waters. Oh man.

I immediately started a bath and relocated the mis-chievous boy, sans his Sunday best, to cleaner waters. In the meantime, the baby sensed he had been abandoned and screamed his displeasure. Our helpful eldest climbed up to him on the changing table to offer comfort, which led to the infant toppling onto the floor and shrieking through a fat, bleeding lip. Why did I even try to go to church? All the effort seemed more frustrating than any worship could ever be worth. But, still, I was determined to get there.

Unfortunately, my frustration level rose faster than I was able to control it. All the bathing, dressing, re-dress-ing, puddle-mopping, and injury-soothing had worn me out completely. Lying out clothes the night before, singing our silly song about cooperation—none of it was any use. But never mind that the wild ones had won. The real battle was not so much with the kids. It was more in my heart.

My heart was pounding, my head was pounding, and I'm sure my face was beet red. You bet I was mad! I was mad that I had to do this alone every week. I was mad that if I ever did get to church, I'd feel scrutinized just because my husband was the pastor. I was mad that I had to get three unruly children into their car seats that barely fit into our compact car while carrying a baby and a diaper bag. But the final straw was when I finally dropped into the driver's seat, reached for my car keys, and realized they were nowhere to be found. I rummaged through my purse. I ran back into the house, noticing, of course, how messy the kitchen was. I cursed. I pleaded with God to help me, a miserable mother who was losing her temper. I told Him I had been beaten by three kids three and under, and the taste of defeat was bitter. My short fuse had totally undone me that morning, and by this time, church was nearly half over. I ran back out to my tethered three, whose only mischief now included smacking at each other while imprisoned in the car. There were my keys, stuck right where I had left them in the driver's door. Stupid me! My anger and frustration had blinded me to their most likely location. I grabbed them and slumped into the seat while my daughter piped up, "Mommy, when are we going to church?"

"Not today, honey," I said as calmly as I could. I looked in my wallet that held five dollars. "Today we are going to buy some cheese instead."

I know it sounds a bit crazy, but we needed cheese. We like cheese for lunch after church, and everyone thought going to buy cheese was a wonderful idea.

As I took cleansing breaths on the way to the store, I had a conversation with God in my head. I told Him I had despaired in the hectic circumstances of the morning. I was impatient and unmerciful to my kids (who were just being kids), and if I made getting to church such hell, they would probably never want to go again. I remembered what it says in Galatians 5:22–23, that "the fruit of the Spirit is love, joy, peace, patience, kindness, goodness, faithfulness, gentleness and self-control." I would try to exercise more self-control in these little moments of mothering anxiety. And if I slipped every now and then, I needed to have patience—with myself as well as with my children. Finding peace amidst a midmorning storm can sometimes seem downright impossible. But if you allow yourself a little leeway, you *can* come out, safe and sound, on the other side.

Over a lovely lunch of cheese sandwiches, my husband asked why we hadn't shown up at church. I smiled and said, "Sometimes you need church, and sometimes you need cheese. I'll explain the rest later."

Be completely humble and gentle;

be patient,

bearing with one another in love.

EPHESIANS 4:2

Be Real

She looked perfect. Her skin was flawless, her clothes were pretty and stylish but not overdone, and her house, husband, and children could not be faulted. To top it off, her kids were athletic, smart, and super-polite, always addressing adults as "Mr." and "Mrs." Her husband was handsome, successful, and exuded a warm, friendly spirit. They seemed to have everything going for them, so it came as a surprise to many when the couple split up and their custody battles grew ugly and vehement. The illusion of blissful domestic life melted away faster than you could say "I do."

But that's just it. The family's perfect appearance was a mirage. Lots of effort had gone into creating the image. We all do it to a certain extent. We aren't always comfortable letting people see how we speak or act inside our kitchens or our vehicles with tinted windows. We carefully craft conversations about our kids to place them in the best light, which in turn is a positive reflection on us. When visiting with a friend, it's easy to share just enough information about us to promote a favorable image.

But to be a friend and really share this path of life and mothering, we have to set aside our pride and let people see us for what we are: human. We can't hold up facades and pretend to be perfect. As much as it's tempting to try to appear put-together, or to have our house look put-together, we all have a junk drawer, a messy closet, and a pile of mismatched socks stuffed away. If you have teenage boys, there may even be places in your home that emit a certain odor.

Just like our homes, our hearts also have disheveled places that we like to keep to ourselves. It's natural to worry that a friend might think less of me if they know how angry I sometimes feel. I have feared being judged by others when they learn that I struggle with gluttony, my temper, impatience, or speeding on my way to work. What if they heard me really out-and-out YELL at my kids? I might not be allowed to write this book! I don't recommend spilling your deepest secrets with lots of people, or with just anyone, but when a trusted, true-blue friend is capable of keeping a confidence, sharing your heart may be a lifeline when life feels impossible. Because now and again, who hasn't fallen short of how one hopes to live and behave?

One Saturday morning when our kids were little, my husband hosted a meeting at our house while I went to work. Before leaving I tidied up the house and put a tray of warm muffins on the table with a vase of fresh-picked flowers. The next day one of the guests told me she had been struck by how orderly and beautiful our home looked when she arrived. She thought I must have drugged our three kids, who were all under the age of four, to create this serene environment. She was impressed. However, what endeared me to her more and what she liked best was finding the kids' cereal bowls in the kitchen sink floating with soggy Cheerios. Then she knew I was a hurried mom just like her, and she felt more at home in my house.

To be perfect is to intimidate; to be human is to encourage! Let down your guard. Be human, not perfect! Connect on the day-to-day struggles. When conversing with a friend, let your spirit relax as you pay closer attention to their words and needs rather than focusing on how you come across. Ephesians 4:2 says, "Be completely humble and gentle; be patient, bearing with one another in love."

Don't even attempt to be like the "perfect family" you may feel enticed to emulate. It's imaginary. Perfect families don't exist, because families are made up of people, and people are imperfect. We all have dysfunctional behaviors that lurk and strain relationships. I know we do in our home, and we're not so different from anyone else.

Rather than waste energy pretending to be better or seemingly better than you are, be real and encourage others to be themselves with you. By allowing your imperfect self to show through, you invite closeness with friends and strangers alike. By sharing the pressures of mothering you may buoy the heart of a sister who will discover she isn't alone.

"For my thoughts are not
your thoughts, neither are your ways
my ways," declares the LORD.
"As the heavens are higher than the earth,
so are my ways higher than your ways and
my thoughts than your thoughts."

ISAIAH 55:8–9

Against All Logic

I'll never forget the August our daughter, Johanna, came home from tennis practice with the news that she'd met an exchange student from the eastern part of Germany, who needed a home for the school year. "Couldn't we please take her?" she asked, as if she'd found a stray puppy. Wow, as if three teenagers in the house wasn't already crazy enough! We told Johanna that we would pray about it, but with the size of our small bedrooms and the busyness of our schedules, we really doubted it. Still, we invited Isa for a Labor Day picnic. That started a fast-rolling ball, and within ten speedy days, Isa moved into Johanna's tiny bedroom (thanks to our boys who relinquished their beds, allowing the girls to have bunks).

That year was especially full—four teenagers coming and going multiplied the phone calls, sack lunches, and trips to the store, and caused a strain on computer time for homework. Then, while Isa was still in her first week of adjusting to life in our home and in America, my mother became unexpectedly and gravely ill, necessitating many flights to Chicago for me to care for her. Working, being mom to four teenagers, and a long-distance nurse for my mother, I felt pretty exhausted much of that year. With many stressors upon us, it made no sense that God would want us to have one more child to parent, but God's logic is not ours, and we had made a commitment to this girl from Germany who wrote "atheist" on her application to study abroad.

My heart went out to Isa, an only child from a quiet home who suddenly joined our hectic family. On top of that, we are a pastor's family, and church and faith were completely foreign to her. After our first Sunday service together, Isa looked at me with huge eyes that communicated complete bewilderment. She respectfully and politely told me that she did not believe in God or Jesus, and she didn't understand how we could. I told her that we didn't require her to believe anything; rather I encouraged her to just hang out with us and our friends. She was a good sport, and continued not only to attend our church, but also another youth group with a friend from school.

During that year I found it difficult to meet everyone's needs as I tried to be mom to four instead of three. My heart clumped along, heavy with grief as it became apparent that my mom's illness was terminal. Still, God graciously gave me enough energy for each day.

At home Isa became a part of our family, yet she resisted our seemingly illogical faith. We talked about cultural differences and spiritual differences, and we discussed how the Church had been oppressed in her former Communist town. She was a very intelligent young woman, full of deep thoughts and excellent questions. I certainly couldn't answer all of them. While I was crying at the thought of losing my mother, she wanted to know why God would allow my mom to suffer. I wasn't able to conjure up any logical response from my place of raw sadness.

All I could do for Isa was love her, be mom for her as best I could, and pray for her. Over nine months she attended many Bible studies, retreats, a missions trip, and joined the softball team at school. In the Spring we could see her softening toward God, and she decided to give prayer a try. Not long after, Isa broke her leg while sliding in softball. Surgery involving a plate and screws followed, as well as lots of time for Isa to sit and heal. While she felt crushed to be laid up, she wisely used the time to search the Bible for answers to her many questions. You know where this leads, don't you?

Isa came to know Jesus and fell completely in love with Him. Very ironically, in the nine months we watched my dear mother's life ebb away, we saw Isa find her new life in Christ. At the end of that school year, we celebrated my mother's life with a beautiful memorial service in Chicago. Two weeks later Isa was baptized in a lovely stream near our home, surrounded by her many friends.

Now, three years later, Isa is in college studying youth ministry. She plans to spend her life leading other teens to faith in a country where many do not yet know Jesus. What seemed completely illogical to us made perfect sense to our all-knowing God. Since we don't have God's wide-vision perspective, we must choose to follow Him with our day-to-day decisions. Retrospect reveals His logic that is far wiser than ours.

The mocker seeks wisdom
and finds none, but knowledge comes
easily to the discerning.

PROVERBS 14:6

The Best Advice

Whether you're a new mom or you've had a houseful for years, it is apparent that mothers are constantly adjusting to new challenges with each stage our children grow into. As we attempt to adjust, advice from others abounds! It starts right away with the first baby. Along with some wonderfully helpful gifts, new moms receive buckets of unsolicited advice. "Schedule the feedings, and in eight weeks you'll be sleeping through the night. Cloth diapers are best. Don't use too many sleeping aids. The babies must learn to pacify themselves. You need a baby sling. Start saving for college." Ack! Soon your head is spinning and you feel overwhelmed.

Here's one tidbit that was passed on to me by a wise woman who saw my confusion when I was bombarded with a deluge of do's and don'ts. As I held our newborn at a baby shower in our honor, she sidled up to me and whispered in my ear, "Tell everyone to mind their own business, and do what you know in your heart is best." I smiled, exhaled, and felt myself relax, realizing hers was the best advice of all. Not wanting to offend our well-wishers, I didn't exactly tell people to mind their own business, but I decided to listen to all advice with a very discerning ear and only apply what made excellent sense to my husband and me.

It wasn't that I thought I knew everything like when I was eighteen. No, I felt quite terrified by my lack of experience in caring for a newborn at home. I had everything to learn and I knew it. I am still grateful for a dear friend who patiently answered my questions about confusing things like the difference between clothes that are sized 24 months and 2T? Or why can't some mothers have dairy products while they are nursing? And what's all the fuss about pacifiers? She and I contemplated when we would give our babies their first solid food. And these questions only multiply when the baby is out of diapers.

Next we make plans for pre-K, kindergarten, and out-of-school activities. Over the years, we help our kids make thousands of decisions as we guide them through high school and on to college, careers, and young adulthood. And wow, do mothers ever have strong feelings about such decisions! Ideas of how children are schooled can lead to divisions amongst tight friends and even within families. It's natural that we gravitate toward those who make similar child-rearing choices, because while the kids are together in school or sports, we parents rub elbows on the sidelines.

The fact is, we constantly receive information intended to help us make sound parenting decisions. Some guidance comes from watching parents whom we admire. Some we glean from the many child-rearing books on the market, or by attending a parenting class. And naturally some emerges from the patterns instilled in our families. However we take our cues for raising children (and here I go giving you more advice), our signals need to be in sync with what we believe God tells us as we talk with Him about parenting. We need to ask Him for clear discernment. As you wade through the piles of parental advice, you'll find much of it is conflicting. Through prayer and conversations with those you trust, you will choose what to accept and what to toss aside.

$\mathcal{M}$ary treasured up all these

things and pondered them

in her heart.

LUKE 2:19

Something to Ponder

I'm sure Mary wasn't the first pondering mother, but she may be the first whose pondering was recorded for all time. Jesus was born on that auspicious night in a humble barn to young parents who couldn't secure indoor lodging. Then, as crazy as it sounds, angels in the sky announced to a gang of shepherds in a nearby field that their Savior had been born in Bethlehem. And they appropriately freaked out. But when the angels told them to not be terrified, they obliged, and excitedly rushed into Bethlehem to find the baby wrapped in clothes and lying in an animal's trough. I imagine a lot of "oohing" and "ahhing" as the shepherds crowded into the barn to see the newborn and his parents. To their amazement, the angel's predictions were correct—right down to the feed box. They took in the sight and then took off to tell everyone about the astonishing events of the night. Just after the shepherds left, Luke 2:19 tells us, "Mary treasured up all these things and pondered them in her heart."

Oh my, she had a lot to treasure and ponder! And really, what mother doesn't? To "treasure" is to realize the enormous value of something and to protect it from harm or loss. Mary didn't want to lose the memories of Jesus' birth and its utterly astounding circumstances. She tried to make sense of these events, turning them over and over in her mind. What a mental challenge Mary encountered as she struggled to understand the events of the previous twenty-four hours, let alone the miracle that led to her pregnancy nine months before. I've always loved that Mary "treasured up all these things and pondered them in her heart." She set a great example for all mothers who, in the throes of mothering, have a lot to try to understand. Granted, none of us have to raise the Son of God, but pondering, carefully thinking, or taking a long, hard look about where we are in the process of raising our children is always good practice.

Pondering is a very personal and internal experience. It includes holding tightly to dear memories of special or difficult times with a child. I remember the evening of our daughter's third birthday party. We had had such a wonderful celebration, and after the party she took my hand and thanked me for the fun. She then added, "The games were great, Mommy!" The party was quite simple and homemade, but to her it was the best ever. I treasured her thankfulness at such a young age. I fell asleep that night pondering our dear daughter's heart and wondering how to keep her from becoming spoiled.

We mothers have much to ponder at all the stages of our children's growing up. Doesn't it make sense that a baby needs frequent feedings to give mothers the chance to sit down and ponder their dear child? Holding an infant while it nurses promotes deep emotional bonds between mother and baby. The intensity of that bond is part of the special, strong relationship that God created for mothers and their offspring. Out of that bond grows a love so deep and dear. When our children are school-age, we wonder at and ponder how they learn new skills and develop talents. When they become teenagers we may ponder how nearly every word we utter is suddenly incorrect and how they grew to know "everything" in their speedy eighteen years!

I invite you to ponder away with me, my fellow moms. As it did for Mary, it leads to praying for our much-beloved children and causes us to rely on God for strength, wisdom, and perseverance. No one can raise a child completely on their own, and pondering and praying can give you energy, strength, and hope. When she "treasured up" and "pondered" all that took place when Jesus was born, Mary taught me that I need a tenacious connection with God. I need to treasure my children. I need to ponder our lives together. And I need to always keep them in my heart.

If you have enjoyed this book

or it has touched your life in some way,

we would love to hear from you.

Please send your comments to:

www.KPTpublishing.com

Bonnie Sparrman is grateful for how being a mother has enriched her life. She and her husband, Eric, have three children of their own and one who joined the family as a German exchange student. Johanna, Bjorn, Karl-Jon, and Isabel, are past the baby-stage, but lessons they taught their parents are worth remembering.

Bonnie is also a registered nurse, writer, culinary instructor, corporate team builder, and consummate baker, who believes that fresh cardamom bread goes a long way to promote friendship and love.

Bonnie is frequently found in the kitchen, welcoming guests—reading, hiking, swimming or cycling the trails that circle the lakes of Minneapolis with her biking buddy, Eric. For Bonnie, a stellar morning is biking to a friend's house with a batch of warm muffins in her backpack.